LET THAT HURT GO

BY
BIANCA MILLER

Library of Congress Cataloging-in-Publication Data

Bianca Miller
Let That Hurt Go
Published by: Bianca Miller Publishing

ISBN: 978-0692152584

10 9 8 7 6 5 4 3 2 1

Printed in the United States of America

Note: This book is intended only as a real life testimony of the life and times of Bianca Miller. Readers are advised to consult a professional before making any changes in their life. The reader assumes all responsibility for the consequences of any actions taken based on the information presented in this book. The information in this book is based on the author's research and experience. Every attempt has been made to ensure that the information is accurate; however, the author cannot accept liability for any errors that may exist. The facts and theories about life are subject to interpretation, and the conclusions and recommendations presented here may not agree with other interpretations.

TABLE OF CONTENTS

INTRODUCTION

Throughout my childhood, I was too young to understand the types of relationships I witnessed in the people around me. It wasn't until I grew older that I realized most of those relationships were toxic. Growing up in that environment caused me to later struggle through my own relationships with men. My mother taught me how to be a lady and respect myself. My father always told me to respect myself and how to deal with men, along with the general lessons he bestowed on me. There are no complaints here; my parents did an amazing job raising me. Although they taught me these lessons, I followed their example; I did what I saw them do. Regardless of how wise their voices rang inside my conscience, I wanted to get out and have my own experiences. After dating for a while, I realized there had to be way more to relationships than what I was going through and what I saw. The relationships and interactions I saw couldn't be real love. I knew there had to be more to it than that. I can't recall anyone I know being completely happy in their relationships. There was always cheating, lying, disrespect and divorce. It's so easy to get caught up in a toxic relationship. Knowing what to expect and look for when meeting someone is essential. Knowing what to do when you see those red flags in someone's behavior or decisions is even more important. The purpose of this true story is to share my own experiences to hopefully prevent other women from suffering through the same trials.

CHAPTER 1
It Went Down in the DM

I met my child's father, Bryson, on April 28, 2015 on Instagram through a direct message (DM). The first two times he tried to talk to me, I shot him down. It was part of the game, and I was still trying to feel him out. One night, he posted an attractive picture with a caption that was basically inviting women to send messages to his DM to talk to him. I fell for it, and we talked late into the evening. I was living in Owego, New York at the time, and he was living in Houston, Texas, our hometown. It was long distance, so we talked on the phone, through text messages, and FaceTimed each other often. He was handsome and charming. I felt myself becoming more and more interested in him.

Talking and texting all day every day helped Bryson and I to get closely acquainted. It was the "honeymoon phase;" you know, that feeling of newness that sends butterflies fluttering through your belly when you first meet someone you really like and everything is going well. Every time he called and checked on me throughout the day, I felt that burst of excitement.

Many times in the courting stage between a man and a woman, it's hard to pace yourself. You meet and everything amazing about that other person is magnified and new. Everything looks like a dream. You're so enamored with this person's attractiveness, smile, intelligence, sense of humor, or how they make you feel that you fail to take a step back and keep a few walls up. When it's long-distance, the allure is even stronger. Think about it- social media is a platform for people to show the best versions of themselves. So, when you stare and drool over a beautiful or handsome picture, you are looking at the retouched, photoshopped version of that individual. You don't see that the person may be only showing you one angle or aspect of his or her life. No one puts their flaws on social media. So when you date online, are you really seeing the true person, or the representation of who that person wants you to believe they are? Is the distance making that person seem even more incredible and attractive? The fact that you can't get to him or her right away-is that what is captivating you?

One day, Bryson's calls and texts suddenly stopped. I reached out to him, and he didn't respond. It was like he abruptly disappeared. Two more days passed. Nothing. I still hadn't heard from him. In my mind, I tried to convince myself that I didn't care. I thought, *to hell with him…who cares if he never responds?* After the first day of his disappearing act, I stopped trying to make contact. On the third or fourth day, he contacted me saying he wasn't going to let me go that easily. Keep in mind that he's the one who disappeared on me, not the other way around.

In June of 2015, I traveled home to visit family for Father's Day, and I finally met Bryson in person. He and I had mutual friends and acquaintances, so I wasn't concerned about the possibility of him "catfishing" me. We spent a few nights together and enjoyed each other's company. I stuck around our hometown for about two weeks, and then it was time to head back to Owego. While visiting, I was so excited to see Bryson that I didn't pay attention to some of the red flags. The first day we saw each other, it was almost like I begged him to pick me up to spend time with him. I allowed my excitement to overshadow the fact that I asked him to pick me up too many times, and he didn't even show up until around midnight.

While I was back in Owego, Bryson had a crazy jealous moment. My coworker, Chris, called with car problems and asked me to pick him up from a store that was about ten minutes away from my home. I was on the phone with Bryson at the time this coworker called. He lost his cool when he found out I was going to pick up a male coworker. He forbade me from picking up Chris. Chris moved to New York alone without any family, so there was no way I was leaving him stranded. I knew what it felt like to live away from family, so I wanted to look out for him. I didn't understand Bryson's problem. I went to rescue my coworker anyway because I wasn't going to allow Bryson to control me, and I didn't care if he agreed or not. He apologized, and I forgave and forgot quickly.

People will show you who they are very early on when getting to know them. You just have to stay observant and not ignore the traits and characteristics that seem small in the beginning but have the potential to become major issues. Red flags are everywhere. They give us those gut instincts we need to make wise and informed decisions. They tell us everything we need to know about people and situations. When in the courting stage, it is almost inevitable that the other person will show you a red flag or two. That's because we're human beings, and all of us have human flaws. These shortcomings don't make someone a bad person - but they send out information. If in the first days or weeks of dating or "seeing" someone, they do something like pull a disappearing act and resurface with no explanation, it has to be assumed that this person has another life somewhere. This person was dealing with another aspect of his or her life that you are not privy to knowing. Huge red flag! You have to determine, as someone who loves yourself, whether that is a deal breaker for you or not. When you ignore the red flag you are sending a message to that other person that you accept the flag and can live with it.

Before I had even met Bryson, I 'd been contemplating the idea of moving back home to Houston. I missed my family and friends. I'm very family-oriented and being all the way in New York was no longer working for me. I officially moved back home in mid-July of 2015. I was so excited to be able to see and spend time with all my family. Plus, Bryson and I were growing more serious; I was a happy woman.

One day, I was hanging out with Bryson and he was talking very aggressively on the phone with his mother. When he hung up, he told me there was a woman who was claiming her baby was his child. I didn't really care if the baby was his or not. As long as he was taking care of this responsibility, doing right by this innocent child, and respecting me, I was cool with it. He told me he didn't believe the baby was his because the mother of the child was sleeping with him and someone else at the same time. He told me he would take a DNA test to find out.

There were a few things I should have noticed. When Bryson posted the picture inviting women into his DM, it was a major red flag. He wanted attention. He wanted to entertain multiple women. He was lost. In truth, I was attracted to him because I was no better than him. I'm woman enough today to admit that. At that time, I felt like I needed a man so badly, and those feelings made me desperate and vulnerable. I was lost. It was cute in the beginning when Bryson wanted to talk to me all day every day, but after a while, his need for constant attention started becoming very annoying. It got to the point that whenever he reached out to me, it was from a place of insecurity. I didn't even want to answer the phone if there were other people in close proximity because I never knew what outlandish remarks he would say. It was embarrassing. I should have addressed the issue in the beginning of the relationship, but I failed to do that. When he went missing for days shortly after we met and got jealous about me helping out a male coworker, I forgave him and things went right back to normal. I know we were not in a relationship during these incidents, but I still should have held him accountable. I should've addressed the situation and let him know exactly how I felt in those moments, but instead, I let him slide. I swept these issues right under the rug.

The insatiable need to be noticed or to be desired is toxic. It leads to uncomfortable or inappropriate interactions that just lead to drama. We all know a person who is obsessed with how many "likes" he or she receives on their social media pages. Think about that. The need for "likes" comes down to the need to *be* liked. Anyone who is so desperate to be liked by people outside of their relationship or gets jealous when their significant other is liked by others, is dealing with a self-esteem issue that will infect and poison the relationship. The need for constant attention comes from a lack of self-love. If you need others around all the time to like you, what does that say about how much you like yourself? All human beings should like themselves enough to not need validation from others, especially not from complete strangers through social media. That type of insecurity is disastrous for a relationship.

CRCRCR

CHAPTER 2
I'm Pregnant

At this point, Bryson and I had only known each other and been dating for about three months. Most nights, I slept over at his place, and naturally, we were "doing some major getting it in." I knew there was a possibility I might've been pregnant, and my body was feeling a little different. I was scared as ever. I didn't know what I was going to do with a baby. I barely even knew this man. I had to figure something out quick.

I went to my cousin, Toya's house for advice. It was her natural reaction to be excited that I could be pregnant, but I was far from excited. We went to a drugstore off the Beltway near Wilson Road and bought a pregnancy test. That one minute waiting on the results was the longest minute of my entire life! The results were negative. I talked to Bryson about it, and we were both relieved. We didn't need a baby in our lives…well, at least not at that moment.

I had been so busy trying to find a new job and get things situated after moving back home that I hadn't made my appointment to get more birth control pills. I had been without birth control for about two months. I finally made my way to the doctor's office. I'd been going to the same clinic for years, so I knew the procedure. At the end of the checkout, the nurse took me back to a private room, asked me which birth control method I preferred and handed me condoms. I knew the routine; I assumed I was about to get my birth control and head out like I usually do. This time, the nurse had her back towards me as she leaned over looking through papers. She then said, "Bianca, it looks like you tested positive for pregnancy, so we're not able to give you birth control." The nurse was still shuffling though papers and hadn't looked back up at me. A few seconds passed, and I still hadn't responded to the news. She finally looked at me. I was crying like crazy! "Aww don't cry! I was 17 years old when I had my first baby. You'll be okay." I was thinking to myself, *Look lady I could care less about what you went through, how old you were when you had your baby, or anything else.* I was old and mature enough to have a child. I wasn't financially stable. Nothing in my life was prepared for the birth of a child, but even still, I knew I would do what I had to do for my child to have a great life.

Riding home, I pondered all the aspects of my life that were about to change. I thought about how I was going to break the news to my parents and Bryson. When I told Bryson through text, he didn't believe me. It wasn't until I took a picture of the paperwork and sent it to him that he got serious. He seemed shocked and asked me if I was going to keep the baby. For me, there was no question; I have nothing against people who get abortions, but I was not raised to use that as an option. I had to woman-up and accept the situation. I laid up and had sex, so I had to accept the consequences.

Bryson kept telling me how he wasn't ready for another baby. He complained about how he didn't have money or time for a baby. I was sick of hearing that mess. I told him to man-up, accept the consequences, or move around. I couldn't listen to that mess anymore. I knew that no matter what happened between he and I, my baby and I would be fine regardless. This is when Bryson's true colors began to show. He began to reveal a side of him I'd never seen before. He was furious that I wasn't going to get rid of our child. He called me a wh*r* and told me he was done with my b*tch *ss. He sent the text in all caps with the iPhone red emoji exclamation marks. I didn't even entertain his tantrum. He sent a few more disrespectful texts, and I ignored him for about a week.

Bryson was the least of my worries; I was trying to figure out how I would to break the news to my parents. My father was out of town, so I decided to tell my mother first. I went to her house and she immediately knew it had something to do with Bryson. Finally, she took a good look at my midsection, and she instantly knew. She said, "Why in the hell would you go do that? You must want to be pregnant!" She had a lot of gripes about the situation, but every day the anticipation and excitement of expecting her first grandchild grew.

As time passed, feelings of unhappiness began to creep into my heart and mind. Here I was pregnant by a man I barely knew, and he didn't even want a child. I began to feel ashamed that I became pregnant by him. If I would've used my head and not have been so hot and desperate for love, I could have avoided this predicament.

My father finally returned home, and I gave him the news. I knew he was bothered by it, but of course he didn't show his true feelings. One thing he was concerned about was how Bryson felt about the whole ordeal. I did not disclose how this man disrespected me, called me out my name and wanted me to have an abortion. Telling my father about Bryson's heinous actions and words would have added fuel to the fire; I just wanted to avoid creating more problems. After telling my parents about my pregnancy, I felt a little relieved like a weight had been lifted off of my shoulders.

When young people put themselves in positions to get pregnant, they rarely think about what it would be like to parent with that other person. You have to be very careful about whom you choose to be the other half of your children. In new relationships where all the deep secrets and information hasn't yet been shared or discovered, it's an unstable position to be in to conceive. It's commonplace to wonder about whether the child will get his eyes or smile, but people need to think more about if the child will inherit his bad habits. And if the child is watching that other parent and learning from the example set by that other parent, how do you stop your child from *becoming* that parent? Children learn how to act and how to treat others based on what they see their parents do and how they see their parents act. When you choose to lay down with someone in a way that could result in a child, would you be comfortable with that person in the bed with you being an example for the child? But no one thinks about that ahead of time. Most people just think about how good the lovemaking feels.

As time passed, Bryson and I seemed to be getting along better. The initial shock of the pregnancy had faded, and after raising a lot of hell, he started to accept that he could not make demands or pressure me into having an abortion. I forgave him for thinking he could control me and for showing me so much disrespect. He was even attending doctor's appointments with me, and for the first time, he seemed to be very supportive. We began rekindling our relationship, spending a lot of time together and enjoying each other. After a long period of toxic fighting and dysfunction, I was actually reconsidering the possibility of us building a future together.

You would think by this point, I would've realized the type of man I was dealing with, but I was nowhere near my breaking point. Not even close! This was just the beginning of all the drama and stress waiting ahead for me. Hindsight is 20/20; If I'd known then what I know now, I would have never even put myself in the situation to get pregnant.

ରେରେରେ

CHAPTER 3
This is Where the Real Problems Started

I got so content and comfortable. The situation of Bryson's disrespect had been placed on the backburner. One day, I was riding with him to my mother's house, and I asked him what he wanted to see happen between us. I figured that either we were going to be in a relationship or not. It was simple. Of course, we decided to be in a relationship. I still had not learned my lesson.

I'd already had a taste of how disrespectful Bryson could be, but this is when his dysfunction reached a point of no return. He became so insecure, disrespectful, emotionally abusive, physically abusive, and all the other traits of a miserable, broken human being! He had a horrible attitude and was very selfish. I became more stressed out than ever before.

He often asked me if any of my ex-boyfriends had reached out to me, if anyone tried to talk to me or flirt with me at work, on social media, or just in general. Even though I'd tell him "no," he always had a response like he just couldn't believe that not one person had approached me with suggestive intentions. At that time, I was telling the truth. He became so jealous and skeptical that I couldn't be open with him. I couldn't share any information regarding other men with him because he made me feel so uncomfortable.

There are so many people in this world in relationships and marriages who are not living in truth. So many people lie about who they are, what they like, what they do and who they know just to avoid dealing with a jealous or judgmental person. That is a type of abuse. No, it's not the same as domestic violence or being physically assaulted, but it's still abuse if you feel you cannot be you. If you can't mention your friends around your man without him getting insecure, or talk to anyone of the opposite sex, you are possibly in a mentally or emotionally abusive relationship. If you have to hide the most harmless things to avoid backlash or conflict in your relationship, you may be in a mentally or emotionally abusive relationship. Remember, insecurity is contagious; one person has it and it negatively affects others around them, sometimes even causing others to be insecure.

Bryson always had an excuse to avoid attending church. So many mornings, he claimed he was too tired or didn't have anything to wear. This was the same man who often bought new clothes to hang out in nightclubs. If he could buy clothes for the club, why couldn't he buy clothes appropriate for church? When we visited one together, he claimed it was too big, or that he knew too many people there and didn't want to attend the same church as them. It was pure bullcrap to me. We tried another church and he claimed something just didn't feel right about the church. We tried other churches too, but he always had some type of excuse. We finally tried a church he liked, which was his brother's church. I liked the church too, but I was mainly happy to just be in a church and hear the Word. Eventually, Bryson started falling into his old habit of finding excuses every weekend to get out of going.

His insecurities, his accusing questions, his horrible attitude, and his controlling behavior continued. At this point, I was about four months pregnant, and I became so stressed. My performance in graduate school was so horrible that I dropped both of my classes. I knew I was going to fail that semester and couldn't afford that loss towards my grade point average. My mind was all over the place and I was on an emotional roller coaster. I lacked the motivation to focus on anything.

Bryson was going to doctor's appointments with me regularly, but there were times I wish he would have just stayed home. He complained about the cost of paying for half of the appointments. Sometimes he complained about even going to the appointments. If he didn't have the money, his frustration would have been understandable. Either way, there was no justification for him to complain about it and create an even more difficult situation. He was just a very difficult person to deal with on top of the stress I already carried.

Bryson's actions were so incomprehensible that I started to feel like he was cheating on me. Why else act so disgruntled about our unborn child? God gives us gut instinct to sense when something isn't right, and it was weighing heavily on my mind. Bryson's level of insecurity was almost unreal. At this point, I didn't even want to be intimate with him at all. He told me if I didn't have sex with him, someone else would. Initially, the thought of him physically involved with someone else bothered me a lot, but then I grew apathetic – I just didn't care anymore. I stopped by his apartment less and less. Some nights, he claimed he was just so tired and didn't want any company, and that was a relief. We were drifting away from each other and reached a point where we would go all day without talking. At one point, it got so bad that we didn't talk for two weeks straight.

I was losing interest fast and was tired of the back-and-forth relationship. For a moment, I considered reaching out to a few of my exes. After pondering my reason for reaching out to them, I realized I was just trying to get the attention and appreciation that Bryson wasn't giving me. I decided to block all of them; Sure, I was looking for that love and affection, but two wrongs don't make a right.

"Baby mama drama" was another problem. Bryson has a total of four children, and the two eldest kids have the same mother. She assumed I had an issue with her because of some gossip she'd heard, but I'd never seen or met the woman. Based on what she thought she knew about me, she told Bryson that I couldn't accompany him to pick up their kids from her house. She claimed I was disrespecting her home by riding with him to pick up the kids. I didn't understand it – it was ludicrous. So, I made a point to get in the car with him to get the kids every time I could. Over time, I noticed Bryson was avoiding picking up his children when I was around. Either he would beat me to it and already have them in his car when I visited, or he would wait until I was busy, in the shower or doing homework before he went to get them. When I confronted him, he admitted he was doing that on purpose to avoid any confrontation between their mother and me. I eventually stopped worrying about it. I didn't go out of my way to tag along; If he was doing wrong, I couldn't stop him. I didn't want to worry about drama. My main goal was to be at peace. I found out he had been texting the kids' mother about personal things and talking to her about inappropriate topics. I was livid; the only thing they needed to discuss was their kids. There was a mountain of drama and headache that came along with the two of them. I began to feel like, *the hell with him, her, and everybody else.* I didn't have time to be worried about such frivolous nonsense.

Sometimes, apathy is your mind's why of making you numb enough to walk away. When you stop caring about what the other person does or says, it's hard to start caring again. This is your sign to exit Stage Left! This is your door to freedom and peace. Unfortunately, most people don't walk through the door. Most people stay on the stage and try to put on an additional show. And then they feel stuck or start to get emotionally involved again. Sometimes it's a fear of change or of not knowing what is out there waiting on the other side. We've all heard people say, "Being single sucks" or "There isn't much out there." This mentality will keep you stuck in the same spot dealing with the same nonsense. So, when you feel yourself starting to get indifferent, that's the time to walk away.

Just when I thought things couldn't get any worse, it got crazier. Bryson and I were hanging out at his house and he asked me If I'd been seeing or dating anyone else. Being so open and honest, I had to tell him the truth. He was enraged! He wanted to know the names of the men I talked to and other details. I tried to explain to him why I even reached out to anyone else in the first place. If he would have been doing his job, no one would could have gotten my attention. He didn't like my response at all. Somehow, he pulled me from the bed, grabbed my wrist and pushed me to the wall. This was in the fifth month of my pregnancy. He was yelling at me being very disrespectful and nasty. He stormed away, still yelling and pissed off. I cried my eyes out, trying to understand how someone could be so cruel. I will never forget some of the things he yelled at me that night. He later apologized over and over, and of course, I forgave him. But deep down, I couldn't shake the feeling of shame I felt for staying with him and putting up with his abuse.

As time passed, Byson told me he had to submit a paternity test. The baby was about five months old around this time. He claimed the mother of the child liked to sleep with multiple men, so he doubted that he was the father. He acted like he hated her. The results came back, and he learned that he was definitely the father. Naturally, more stress was added to my plate. More weight was placed on my shoulders. Months passed, and I hadn't even seen the baby. I started to get concerned as to why he hadn't seen his son. His story was that the mother wouldn't allow him to see the baby. The baby's birthday approached, and I asked Bryson if he called, checked on him, or even tried to get him a gift. His response was that every time he called the child's mother, she never answered the phone. He even attempted to call her in front of me and she didn't answer. I didn't understand why he was paying child support if he couldn't even see his child. It made no sense to me. After the baby's birthday passed, he told me the child's mother changed her phone number and he wasn't able to reach her at all.

Time passed, and we settled into a comfort zone. We were getting along for the most part, although he still asked insecure questions here and there, but I dealt with it. I was fighting the nagging feeling of knowing something was missing; I was not completely happy with him and hated the feeling of settling.

It didn't help that his social media existence was full of females commenting on his pictures. He loved taking pictures and posted them often, but it was never pictures of us. He was so showy and vain with his posted photos, but he did not proudly show his family. His excuse was that he didn't want people to know his business. When he finally posted pictures of us, he claimed he didn't want to tag me because he didn't want other men to know my identity. He claimed that tagging me would just lead to men he knew trying to approach me. I knew these were excuses, and I was so tired of his social media accounts that I eventually blocked him, and he's been blocked ever since. I didn't want to be bothered with any of it.

His friends were another issue that caused strife in our relationship. I didn't care for them at all. If he truly wanted to make a complete change, he would've had to distance himself from those friends. He shared stories with me often about his friends cheating, abusing their girlfriends, bragging about materialistic things, and resorting to other negative behaviors that showed immaturity and disrespect. How can you make a life change if you're constantly surrounded by negative energy? How can that sort of association build positive character? Every time he told me he was going to hang out with his friends, I felt uncomfortable. It didn't help that he frequently wanted to go out with his friends, but rarely ever took me anywhere.

Over time, things went from bad to worse. Although I didn't plan to be pregnant, I often thought about what life would be like if I was pregnant by someone else. My life was full of disorder and disappointment. I was supposed to have a gender reveal party, but I didn't even want it. In fact, I had no desire to even have a baby shower. Dealing with the negativity in my relationship infected every other area of my life.

In retrospect, I realized I somewhat forced Bryson into a relationship. I know I can't force another human being to do anything, but I was the one who brought up the idea of being in a relationship. Bryson simply went along with the flow. God spoke to me long before things had gotten that far. I didn't listen, so I continued to face mistreatment and misery. God kept saying, "Run while you can," but I didn't heed Him. What I didn't understand at the time was that there was no way he could love and respect me, because he didn't love and respect himself. There was no way the mothers of his children would respect me because he didn't respect me. He was so insecure because he wasn't sure about himself as a man. I sometimes look back and laugh at the way I allowed his social media to bother me so much. Those things that bothered me so much on social media only happened and continued to happen because he allowed it. His friends were just a reflection of him.

People will treat you the way you allow yourself to be treated. Most young people in relationships either don't know this, or don't have the courage to test it. You have to have some non-negotiables; there have to be some aspects of the relationship where you will not budge. Make a list now of your non-negotiables, and stick to them. For some people, cheating would be on the list. That means that if the other person cheats, you're out the door. For others, cheating may be forgivable through disclosure and counseling. No one can tell you what you should and should not tolerate. Only you can do that. You have to look in the mirror and decide what you can live with accepting. So, if cheating is a non-negotiable, and your man cheats, you have to be okay with walking away. If not, you will send a message that you are definitely that chick to be cheated on. You will send a message that he can run around town, getting into other women's beds, come home and get in the bed with you, and you will not leave. Knowing that will make him comfortable with continuing to do it because you have made it negotiable, not a deal breaker. If talking to you disrespectfully is something you put up with time and time again, it will get worse, and even more disrespectful. He will gain confidence while you get more insecure. He will get bolder, while you get quieter. Because every time he does something and gets away with it, he has won the negotiation.

ଉଉଉ

CHAPTER 4
The Heartbreak

On May 8, 2016 I was sitting on Bryson's sofa when I began to have contractions. When I told him it was time to have the baby, he thought I was joking and being dramatic. I was riding on the passenger side of my Camaro on the way to the hospital, and the discomfort grew more intense. When I got to the hospital, the nurses told us that I was already six centimeters dilated. The pain started getting worse and worse. My original plan was to have a natural birth without anesthetics, but things changed quickly! I took the medicine the doctors gave me with no hesitation. Every time I pushed or had a contraction, my baby's heart rate would drop. In the end, I had to have an emergency C-section.

My son was born on May 9th. My relationship with Bryson was so stressful that it affected my ability to bond with my son. Each time the nurses and visitors walked out of my room, I cried. Every time Bryson left the hospital, I cried. I felt alone and lacked that connection with my son that I assumed was automatic. Some people may call it post-partum depression, but I thought differently. The toxic relationship I was in made everything else in my life difficult. I didn't feel supported or cared for the way a new mother should be treated.

After giving birth, I recovered at my parents' home. I didn't know much about caring for an infant. My mother taught me how to change my son, feed him, bathe him, and a lot of other aspects of mothering I needed to learn. At about two weeks post-partum, I went to stay with Bryson for a while. Things were going pretty well; we took turns getting up in the middle of the night to care for our son. I stayed home all day with our son while Bryson worked. I began to enjoy that time alone with the baby. The bond I felt was once missing began to grow stronger and stronger. I started to feel like a real mother.

One day, my son and I were sleeping, and a loud knock at the front door woke me up. It was so loud that I thought it was best to call Bryson. I asked him if the maintenance man was supposed to come by that day or if he was expecting anyone. He said no, so I carefully made my way down the stairs, still sore from my surgery. I looked out the window near the front door, and I saw a female sitting in a gray four-door sedan talking on a phone. She was looking right at me. She came to the front door. We were standing face-to-face. She told me her name was Ashley and that she was Bryson's son's mother. This was the son he claimed to never see.

I invited her inside so we could talk. According to Ashley, Bryson had been seeing his son often, spending nights with her, and sleeping with her since I've known him. She'd been to Bryson's apartment several times. She revealed so many of his lies. She seemed very mature and gave me so much information that my head was spinning. She saw our baby and the pictures of Bryson and me on the nightstands on each side of the bed. She was shocked and told me the pictures were never there when she came over to see him. She was even more shocked when she found out that I spend time with Bryson and his older children regularly. She told me she felt ashamed, and that it all made sense as to why he was never with her for holidays, and why she never got to spend time with his other children. She knew all along that something wasn't right, but she couldn't quite put her finger on it. While we were sitting and talking, Bryson called me and I didn't answer. We continued to talk and he FaceTimed me again. He was trying to figure out who was at the door. I turned the phone camera around on FaceTime so he could see her, and she waved at him. In shock, he quickly hung up the phone. She got up abruptly and told me she had to leave because she knew he was going to be on his way there. We exchanged numbers. She left in such a rush as if she was afraid of him.

I was lost. I was sitting on the sofa crying. I didn't have the strength to even move. I knew something wasn't right, but I didn't know it was that bad. Just when I thought we were healing and growing as a family, I was hit with this revelation. I was going back and forth with myself, trying not to believe all of it was true. But deep down, I knew she wasn't lying because the things she said about Bryson had his name written all over them. There was nothing he could say to convince me that everything she said was a lie. She wanted to be with him so badly that she made a point to walk up to his front door to reveal all that stuff about him. I guess her plan and ultimate goal was to destroy our relationship so she could have him for herself.

Twenty minutes after hanging up on me, Bryson came home. He busted in the door screaming, asking me where she was like he was going to beat her up or something. I was still sitting on the sofa crying. He was yelling at me, asking me if I was going to leave him. He was acting like I was the one who did *him* wrong. He kept asking questions, trying to figure out exactly what she told me. He started throwing things around the house. He was yelling at the top of his lungs and the baby started crying. He threw about three or four full jugs of baby water in my direction all while I was holding our baby. I called my father to pick me up because I didn't trust Bryson at this point. It was pouring down raining outside. Bryson told me to go stand outside and wait for my father. The last thing I wanted to do was fight with him while I had my three-week-old son, not to mention, I was only three-weeks postpartum and still recovering from a C-section. I was headed towards the door and he stopped me from going outside. He told me to tell my family to hurry up and come get me. I couldn't stand being there any longer. My father lived further away than my mother. I called my mother and she arrived quicker. Bryson aggressively helped carry my things and the baby's things out of the house. He seemed to not care about a thing. Not one time did he apologize. Not only was he kicking me out, but he was kicking his own son out too. I'll never forget the level of disrespect he showed that day in the things he said and did to me.

My mother drove my son and me home in the bad weather. Being on the road was the last place we should have been in the middle of a rainstorm. The situation was so messed up, and I had no idea he was cheating. Looking back on it, I should've known from all the red flags he showed me. He obsessively asked me who I'd been talking to or if anyone tried to talk to me. I later realized he asked these things because *he* was doing wrong. He never believed I was being 100% faithful to him, even though I never gave him reason to be suspicious. Although I never dressed inappropriately, he always had criticism about my attire. He was so concerned and jealous because he knew he was doing wrong and was afraid it would happen to him too.

He repeatedly called and texted me all night. I didn't expect things to turn out the way they did. I was so hurt. I was depressed. I just wanted to lay in bed all day and night and do nothing. I finally answered one of his calls, and he just continued to lie. He kept denying cheating on me with Ashley. She told me he came to spend the night with her while I was recovering from my C-section at my mother's house. I couldn't believe he was still lying about the situation. I decided to call Ashley for proof. She sent me screenshots of text messages from the last time he went to her home. In the messages, he repeatedly asked her if he could come to her house. He basically begged to go to her house. My heart was racing as I read the truth to all his lies. The same night he was begging her to let him come over was the same night he stopped responding to my messages and claimed he went to sleep. The morning after, I remembered how he called me fussing about how I didn't try to wake him up. Then he accused me of dealing with another man that night, the same night he spent with Ashley and pretended to be sleep at his own home. What makes his accusations more ridiculous is that I was recovering from a serious operation and could barely move. He tried to flip the whole situation as if I was the one doing wrong. All along, he stopped responding to my text messages to go be with her!

Some people can't admit to being guilty, even when they are caught red-handed. They would rather deflect the attention away from themselves and onto what someone else did. They won't accept their wrongdoing and try to make it right. They will deny, deny, deny, and when you are angry or hurt by what they did, they will get even angrier and lash out. People like this seem like they're trying to avoid facing you, but they are really avoiding facing themselves. Everything is always someone else's fault, and they lack the maturity to maintain adult relationships. This type of person will be so adamant of their own innocence that they'll have you looking at yourself as if you are the one at fault. Much of it comes from pride – simply being too indignant and proud to just admit being wrong. It requires a great deal of humility and maturity to own up and say, "I was wrong."

I was home and on maternity leave for the next six weeks, so I had nothing to do to occupy my mind and time. Besides taking care of the baby, I constantly thought about how Bryson played me. I tried to keep busy to take it off my mind, but nothing worked. I forgave him for what he did, but I just couldn't believe he treated me like that. As time went on, we talked more and more over the phone. Bryson hadn't seen our son in a while. I wasn't keeping his son away from him or forbidding him from seeing his own child, but it was difficult to look at Bryson or even to be in the same room with him. Every time I looked at him, I was sickened just thinking about how trifling he was as a man. It took me some time to look at him or talk to him without immediately thinking about what he'd done.

Bryson apologized to me just about every day, or even multiple times a day about what he'd done. I started to heal and began spending time with him more and more. I eventually decided to give him another chance. He appeared to have gotten his act right. He wanted to be back in a relationship, but of course I was hesitant. I needed more time to think about being back with him. A few weeks later, I decided I would be with him since he seemed to be maturing and making positive changes. One of my requirements to be in a relationship with him was to move in with him. At that time, I felt we could only build if we were in the same household. He agreed for me to live with him.

My father, Bryson, and I moved all my things to Bryson's apartment. I was excited and very happy to be moving with him. Things were going pretty smoothly. Bryson was becoming increasingly supportive and passionate. By this time, I had developed a great relationship with Bryson's two oldest kids. I enjoyed spending time with the kids when they visited, and we were all attending church together on some Sunday mornings. Sometimes we even went on family outings together.

Just when I thought things couldn't go sour, they did. I had major trust issues. I didn't trust Bryson at all. He had lied about so many things, even about his son to cover up his cheating. I had a feeling he was still lying or hiding something, but I just couldn't put my finger on it. Anytime I asked him anything related to him cheating, he'd become enraged. Since the day I found out about his wrongdoings, he refused to talk about any of it. I knew I wasn't going to be satisfied until I found out why he did it, if he was on child support or not, how long he'd known her, if she knew about me all along, and lots of other questions. I wanted specific details and felt that discussion was necessary to put my mind at ease, allowing us to grow and build trust.

The tension between us was stifling. It was tearing us apart, and it showed me that the two of us living under the same roof was a huge mistake. He complained about every little thing. If things didn't go his way, he flipped out into a full tantrum. He talked so much - it was unreal. But it wasn't simply the talking that was the problem. It was the negative things he talked about that bothered me so much. He was so confrontational and couldn't accept being wrong. He was a terrible listener. If we had an argument, he would go on and on about the same thing repeatedly. The way our conversations went showed me how he was not ready to love me; he still had entirely too much growing to do. Every time he came home from work, I wished he would have stayed gone longer. His job was another problem. He was a barber, so there was always some rumor or drama about him and different females. Countless, random chicks would just show up at the barbershop because his work location was listed on his social media accounts. How can there be trust in this sort of environment? The only thing that kept me in the relationship with him was the hope for what I imagined could be between us.

His social media accounts were the root of most of my complaints because the content and interactions were blatantly disrespectful. When he looked at my social media accounts, he didn't see men commenting and leaving hearts and other flirty emojis under my pictures. If I ever got an inappropriate comment from someone, I deleted it. I felt he needed to show the same level of respect, but I had to learn that everybody is not the same. I can't expect others to handle affairs the same as I would. We're not celebrities or public figures, so we have control over what is posted on our accounts. At some point, he said he understood my feelings and the principle of it all. He told me he'd gotten rid of all his social media accounts so that we could focus on building our relationship.

Most days were bad, but a few of them were good. The pleasant days and moments are what kept me going. It seemed as if Bryson had more trust issues than me. The way he constantly questioned me, one would think that I was the one who had the history of cheating and lying. He was clearly only acting like that because he was either afraid that I was going to cheat, he was cheating again at that moment, or he was contemplating cheating. It was one of those reasons, a combination of them, or all of them that plagued his mind. One of the most irritating things about our relationship was his need to know where I was all the time. Knowing my location wasn't the problem; his crippling insecurity was the issue that was destroying our relationship. I hated it with a passion. I had a nagging feeling he was still being disloyal. One day, he got angry that I didn't let him know I was going out to get food. I went to get the food and came right back home. I couldn't take the accusations and bickering anymore, so I suggested we turn on the location feature on our cell phones. This way, he would no longer have to ask me about my location – he could just look at his own phone and see for himself. That way, we would always know each other's location. He was vehemently against it. He didn't like the idea of being monitored and treated like a child. He fussed and cursed about it, but we still ended up doing it. I knew he had to be up to something, because if he wasn't, he wouldn't have responded that way. Over time, we argued so much that we turned our locations on and off often. We eventually abandoned the idea because it was ineffective since we both did not leave it on as a constant.

Bryson claimed he wanted me to trust him, so we agreed to register our fingerprints on each other's phones so they could be unlocked at any given moment. It wasn't my style to snoop through other people's business, so I never even exercised my ability to look though his phone. One morning, I heard what sounded like footsteps, and I turned over in the bed. Bryson was standing at the side of the bed near the nightstand where my phone sat. He appeared to be touching something on the nightstand, and then he quickly handed me an envelope of our son's pictures from a recent photoshoot. I was so confused, trying to figure out why he was handing me those photos so early in the morning. I glanced at my phone on the nightstand and then looked at him. Right then, I knew he'd been looking through my phone, but he tried to distract me with the pictures. He insisted he didn't look through my phone, but I knew better. What he failed to understand was that I didn't have a problem with him having access to my phone, but sneaking and going through my stuff was an issue. Even after that happened, I still didn't feel the need to go through his personal belongings.

Bryson asked me if he could go to his friend's pool party. He had been staying in the house quite a bit and not hanging out as much, so I was okay with him going. He went to buy a new outfit and shoes for the party. Bryson loved to stay in touch with me by talking to me and texting me all day. Every time he went out with his friends, he would text me periodically. I always encouraged him to just have a good time with his friends and talk to me later. For some reason, he never took that too well and always made a point to stay in touch with me while away. I had mixed feelings about his need to do this. In a way, I liked it, but on the other hand, I knew it was coming from a place of insecurity, and I just wanted him to leave me alone. All of his friends were womanizers, so I didn't trust them at all. Besides, you know what they say: "Birds of a feather flock together." At around 11:00 pm that evening, his texting started to slow down. I waited a while to hear from him, and then I Face-Timed him. He answered, but all I could hear was loud music and people. I figured if I waited a few minutes, he would go outside to call me. I waited…but received no call. I Face-Timed him again, and when he answered, all I could see was dark screen on my phone and I heard the loud music and DJ again. I let a few minutes pass by before I decided to call him again, but he didn't answer. At that time, we had the location feature activated on our cell phones, so I could see exactly where he was located. I called my mother and asked her to watch the baby for a little while. I got dressed in less than thirty minutes. Bryson drove my car to the party, so I was left with the Buick he'd purchased about three weeks prior that was already having car problems. None of that was on my mind.

I was so focused on going to see what he was up to, because I didn't trust him.

My mother lived less than ten minutes away. I was dropping off my son when Bryson called me. He told me he was on his way home. I was upset that I didn't get to go to the party and bust him.

Bryson and I arrived home around the same time. His clothes were soaking wet. Why in the world would he drive my car in soaking wet clothes? Judging by the look on my face, he knew I was pissed. He told me the reason I couldn't see him on the phone was because his phone was in his backpack, but his Bluetooth was on his ear. Of course, I didn't buy it. He removed the wet clothes and left them on the floor. He was staggering around and slurring his words. I couldn't believe he was so intoxicated that he couldn't talk or walk properly. In my opinion, it was all a front just to avoid the conversation about him not showing me his face on FaceTime. He clearly was trying to get out of talking about what he was doing at the party. Just watching him do all that faking pissed me off even more. He flopped on the couch and went to sleep snoring loudly.

I was sitting on the other side of the couch watching TV when I saw Bryson's phone light up. I wanted to grab his phone so bad, but I talked myself out of it. The phone lit up again a few minutes later. My fingerprint was still registered on the phone, so I knew had access to its contents. He was snoring so loud, and I knew he wasn't going to wake up anytime soon. I grabbed the phone and went into his room. I looked through the text messages, call logs, and emails. I didn't find anything in the phone, but I saw a picture of him in his photo gallery that stood out to me. I could tell he used Snapchat to take the picture. He'd supposedly deleted all his social media accounts. I downloaded the Snapchat app on his phone. He used the same username for everything, so figuring it out wasn't rocket science. I reset the password using his email and I was able to log into his account.

There were so many women he'd been talking to on Snapchat. Women had sent him revealing pictures. Some of the women he'd just talked to within the last few hours. One of the women was the mother of his child. He'd previously claimed to not have contact with her at all. I was so pissed off that I woke his butt up. When I told him I saw his little video he'd just posted on Snapchat, he lied immediately. He told me he was on his friend's Snapchat account. I showed him all the stuff I found, and he couldn't deny it.

Once again, he acted like I was the one who did wrong. He got so pissed off and didn't want to own up to his own mess. He was yelling and cursing. I never met someone so disrespectful. He got so angry that he got my phone and looked through it. He was even more upset when he couldn't find anything incriminating in my phone.

It blew my mind to know that this man deleted his social media apps before he returned home. The lying was no surprise, but to go through the trouble of downloading and deleting accounts was like living a double life. He knew by the look on my face that I was just tired of dealing with him. After he finished cursing and yelling, he started his begging spree. Every time we got into a similar situation, he'd always resort to begging me to stay with him. I didn't promise to stay, but I didn't leave either.

Time passed by, and I was so uncomfortable in the same house with him. There was so much tension between us. First, I found out about the cheating, and then the social media mess. Where did he draw the line? Where would it end? I was tired of waiting around for him to get his act together. I told him what I needed from him. I told him what was acceptable and what was not acceptable. We discussed all the things that needed to change as soon as possible in our relationship in order to try to make it work.

As usual, things seemed to be improving and were temporarily going well. Ashley broke down and told me that Bryson had met her one day at a dollar store near his apartment around the same time I found out Bryson was lying about social media accounts. If it wasn't one thing, it was another. Just when we'd get into what seemed to be a healthy groove, old habits and issues would resurface. I didn't know how many more lies I could take.

I told Bryson I was leaving him. I started packing my things to leave. He pulled down some of my clothes hanging up in the closet and threw them all on the floor. He took my shoeboxes and threw them to the floor. He was really showing out! One minute, he'd begged me to stay, and the next minute, he demanded that I leave. Before I knew it, he had me pinned up on the wall in the restroom threatening to hit me. I tried my best to get him to let me loose, but I couldn't overpower him. I didn't realize how tight of a grip he had on my arm until he let me go and I felt a relief. I looked down and saw blood on my arm from his fingernail digging into my skin. As he was walking out of the restroom he started kicking the belongings I'd packed on the floor toward me. He continued cursing me out and yelling at me as he was kicking my things at me. He finally left the room. He went to his kid's room for a while and then came back into the room where I was packing and he started crying.

I didn't have to second guess about moving out this time. I rented a U-Haul and took all of my things and my son's things from the apartment. It was such a relief not to be around negativity all day every day. He begged me to stay, but I wasn't having it. From that day forth, I knew I'd never make the mistake of moving in with him again.

I forgave Bryson for the things he said and did to me. I even started going over to his apartment to stay for a few nights and then I'd go back home. It was inconvenient packing for a few nights all the time and going back and forth, but it was better than living with him.

Since I didn't leave when God showed me all I needed to know, I got hurt more and more. Men like Bryson are not ready to stand up and take responsibility. They are not yet adequate to build lives with real woman. They want girls they can deceive, misuse and abuse. Moving in with him was not doing it God's way. I asked for trouble. I constantly took him back without seeing a real concrete change. This is a cycle that most women get caught repeating. They make decisions based on a man's words rather than his actual actions or evidence. I had to ask myself, *how many times do I have to get abused to realize that Bryson and I are just not on the same page?* When you have to snoop through phones, that means there's trust issues. At that point, it's either time to leave or time to work on fixing the trust issues.

Jealousy and insecurity are like toxic waste. They serve no purpose in a relationship except to infect the way people think, interact, react and treat each other. Some people justify the jealousy by saying they want transparency, and that's why they share each other's phone passcodes and account passwords, but if you are in a relationship where you feel the need to reveal every part of your day and life just to keep the other person from going crazy, you are living in a warped reality. That is not love. That is not even *like*. People who have true friendship and true love do not have to do that. There should be no need to snoop or follow someone to catch them in the act. What kind of quality of life is that? To never be able to relax and trust that the person you love is doing the right thing when he or she is away from you? To always suspect that there is some kind of scandal happening behind your back? Why live like that? The truth is that some people only know suspicion and scandal. Some people have witnessed only distrust and disloyalty. So that's all they know. It leads to emotional distress that's difficult to manage. When you see someone who can flip emotions like a light switch, who is angry and spewing hate at one moment and then crying and begging you to stay the next moment, it has nothing to do with you. These are the signs of deep-rooted emotional baggage that a person drags from place to place, and from relationship to relationship. This person has too much pride to admit to the baggage, so it just builds and builds until it's too heavy to carry and spills over irrationally. This person is not equipped to build a life with another person. This person is not in a good enough space to bring anything to another person's life except turmoil, strife and confusion.

 beta beta beta

CHAPTER 5
The Problems Continued

Bryson and I went to Nikki's house together to pick up his kids. The kids were already in the car when Nikki came outside. Bryson and I were parked on the side of the street and we heard Nikki saying, "I told you not to disrespect my house." Bryson and I both pretty much knew she was talking about me. By that point we assumed she'd accepted that I was in the picture, and she was no longer throwing a fit about me being with him when he picked up his kids, but I guess not. Bryson got pissed off and they started arguing. They were cursing each other and yelling in front of the kids. I looked in the backseat to see Bryson's daughter crying. At that point, I tried to stop Bryson and get him to cut it out in front of his kids, but he didn't budge. In the middle of the argument, Nikki mentioned that Bryson was jealous of the boyfriend she had at that time. She said Bryson sent her texts saying he missed her. Bryson told her to prove that he sent text messages saying that. She retrieved her phone and began searching for the messages. I asked her to show them to me. When I glanced at Bryson, he seemed a little shaken up. I'd been dealing with him long enough to know when he was lying. After seeing the look on his face, I didn't have to look at her phone to know he' d done something inappropriate. While searching through the phone, I didn't actually see the text where he told her he missed her, but I did see texts where he'd ask her opinion on my son's name, or on a new table he was considering for his apartment. I couldn't understand why her opinion mattered so much, especially on something as personal as what I wanted to name my son. It was too friendly and close for comfort. On top of that, they argued like they were a couple in a relationship. It left a nagging feeling inside me.

Weeks after this incident, Bryson explained that he told Nikki he missed her in a friendly way. He must have thought I was a complete fool. I didn't buy that bogus explanation at all, and it didn't even make sense. If the tables had been turned, he would have lost his mind. If I'd said I told someone I used to date that I missed them, whether in an innocent "friendly" way or not, he would've thrown a fit.

Just listening to the two of them argue made me think about all the unnecessary drama that comes along with being in a relationship with Bryson. I already didn't trust him, and adding constant conflict to our situation didn't help at all. Every time he dealt with his ex, my mind would spin; I always wondered if he was really just picking up the kids or if he was getting the kids and being involved with her inappropriately too. He had my mind all screwed up. I even found out he deleted a few text messages between the two of them. Looking through his phone, I noticed the texts and times didn't add up. He'd deleted some texts he didn't want me to see.

As time passed, I grew more and more unsettled with the feeling that our relationship just didn't feel right. I knew Bryson was doing wrong, but I just couldn't put my finger on it. When I asked him about the son he supposedly never gets to see, he got angry. His reaction alone created the suspicion that he was still dealing with his son's mother. It was strange for him to get irritated just from being asked about his child. Ashley didn't allow Bryson to pick up the child or go to her place to visit...at least that's what Bryson told me. He claimed to have attempted to reach out to her several times but she always turned him down. I didn't understand the situation; he was paying child support and had rights, so why wasn't he seeing his son? All of it just made me grow more and more suspicious. Deep down, I had a feeling that Bryson was just lying about Ashley not allowing him to see their child just so he could continue to deal with her on his terms.

There was no way I could take Bryson's word for it anymore; I didn't believe a thing he said. I decided to take matters into my own hands and reached out to Ashley myself. When I called her, she was at work and told me that we could talk at two o'clock that day. A little after one o'clock, she sent me a long text. In that text, she was nasty and disrespectful. She claimed that she slept with Bryson about two months prior and he begged her to get a Plan B emergency contraception pill. After reading that text, I was so pissed off that I couldn't concentrate. I stood in the locker room at work with my heart was beating so fast and I called her. She sent me to voicemail. I tried to call her again, and she blocked my phone number. I was so angry that my hands were trembling, making it almost impossible for me to use my phone properly. I called Bryson to confront him, and of course, he denied it. I hung up on him and his lies and sat down for a minute to calm down. When I went back to my desk, it took me a few minutes to relax before I could function well enough to do my job.

I didn't want to believe Bryson had the audacity to do that, but I knew from his response that he was lying. He was the type of liar who would go on and on to try to prove his lie is the truth, only making himself sound more dishonest.

When I arrived at his house that day, he tried to avoid me, but he knew I wasn't going to let him off the hook that easy. I asked him about Ashley's claims and he denied them again. I made him call her right there in front of me to prove he did not sleep with her. He called her, and he spoke to her with so much disrespect. He called her a liar and accused her of just wanting to sabotage our relationship and break us up. Listening to her, I could sense that she was shocked at what he was saying. She eventually hung up in his face and blocked him from calling and texting her. She didn't know I was there with Bryson during the conversation she'd just had with him. After she hung up on him, she texted me. I don't remember the conversation word for word, but I do remember one thing she said that stuck out. She compared dealing with Bryson to dealing with the devil and she said she hoped I catch my head and get away from him as soon as possible. Still, the fact that Bryson called her gave me just little comfort. In my heart, I didn't believe him, but I didn't have evidence, so I stayed in a relationship with him.

It was Christmas time and I was very excited. Bryson and I agreed that we would buy gifts for the kids and celebrate Christmas together like a family. I was super excited about picking out gifts for the kids. We bought a tree and took the kids to Walmart to help pick out holiday decorations for the tree and the apartment. We had a blast putting up the tree and hanging the ornaments. The kids were so excited, and I loved every minute of it.

Bryson told me he knew a guy that could get the kids gifts for a good discount. All he had to do was pay the guy and he would hook us up with all the presents the kids wanted. Two weeks before Christmas, Bryson still didn't have the gifts. He tends to wait until the last minute to take care of things, so I constantly reminded him that Christmas was right around the corner. A week before Christmas, he still hadn't brought home the gifts. He told me not to worry about it, and that he would take care of it. Three days before Christmas, there were still no gifts. Something wasn't right. I talked to my mother that day and she was telling me how glad she was that the kids finally got their gifts. I was confused. My mother has a close relationship with Bryson's kids and talked to them on the phone quite a bit. My mother claimed she was talking to the kids on FaceTime and Bryson's son showed her an airplane, which was one of his Christmas gifts. Bryson's son wanted an airplane so bad, and it was the most important gift to him on his Christmas list. Deep inside, I suspected up Bryson was up to his old sneaky ways again. When I confronted Bryson and asked why he didn't tell me he'd already gotten the Christmas gifts, he said he hadn't gotten any gifts yet and was waiting on the guy with the discount to give him the gifts. Later that same day, Bryson said he was going to meet the guy in the Walmart parking lot to get the gifts. He Face-Timed me on his way to meet the man, and he called me on his way back home. I asked him if the man was able to get his son's airplane for a discounted price, and he said "yes." Bryson had no idea I already knew the kids had some of their gifts, but I decided to keep that knowledge to myself, just so I could catch him in a lie. I asked Bryson if they had received any gifts prior to him meeting up with that guy, and he said "no." The next day, I had to go to work and I needed to find some excuse to go to Bryson's house. Due to the holiday, it was busy day at his job, so I knew he would be getting home late. I had access to his apartment, but I didn't want to go there without him knowing. I left work to head for his place, and called him when I was two minutes away to let him know I was going there to pick up our son's extra car seat. Bryson immediately told me his mother had borrowed the car seat for his newborn nephew. I went to his house anyway just to see what gifts were there, if any. When I arrived and walked into the apartment, the first thing I saw was my son's car seat. He lied about that. Why would he lie? He wanted to keep me away from the apartment for some reason, and I was going to find out one way or another. I examined the gifts near the Christmas tree. There was no airplane in the pile of gifts. He'd told me gave the man $1,000 to spend on gifts, but what I was looking at appeared to be worth about $300. Bryson had to be lying about a few things.

On my way home, I called Bryson to give him a piece of my mind. Of course, he continued lying and denying everything, like always. After revealing all that I knew, he couldn't deny the truth. He admitted he lied about the whole situation. He'd given his child's mother some money to buy the gifts. The night he said he met the guy to get the gifts, he'd met his kids' mother to get some of the gifts so that the kids would have presents to open at both his house and her house. That pissed me off for a few reasons. I had been excited to go pick out the gifts with Bryson and the kids, so my feelings were hurt. But, my main problem was all the lying about the whole thing. I had no problem with the fact that he gave her money for the kids, but he hadn't even made sure my son and I had everything we needed before giving out money. He hadn't given me any money for our son, nor did he even attempt to get something for the son he didn't see. If he would've communicated with me throughout the ordeal, everything might have been okay. If it was a financial issue, I would've understood that. Instead, he lied, and he told me I think he's supposed to be perfect and not make mistakes. He was so full of it that I hated to hear him talk sometimes. According to Bryson, he'd made an agreement with his children's mother to provide gifts for the kids, and I wasn't supposed to know. This incident became another reason why I didn't trust their relationship.

At this point, I couldn't even stand to be around Bryson, and I decided to spend Christmas without him. My son and I went to my cousin's house instead, along with other family members. Typically, I have the most fun when I'm with my family, but I wasn't having fun at all. I was so depressed and hated I had to spend Christmas without him.

When we began communicating again, I just couldn't let it go. I let out all of my anger over everything he'd done and how much I saw him as a sorry excuse. He finally admitted he had sex Ashley, his second oldest son's mother. This was the same girl and same incident he lied about months earlier. In my heart, I never believed him from the start. He also revealed that he'd visited the baby a few times without me knowing. He apologized to me repeatedly.

By this time in the relationship, there was no way I could let my guard down and try to trust this man. I began to hate everything that came out of his mouth. His words weren't worth hearing. My resentment grew tremendously, and I became so rude towards him. He noticed how rude I became because I had always been so nice to him and would hold my tongue. He had always known that hurting him was the last thing I wanted to do, but those days were over. With each passing day, I cared less and less. I didn't believe a thing he said to me. I found myself developing self-esteem issues. I was just so hurt about everything. I began to wonder if I was not enough for him, or if he was no longer attracted to me because of the weight I'd gained from our baby. He made me feel so low.

Unfortunately, when dealing with a toxic and dysfunctional relationship, the part that is damaged the most is what most people can't see with the naked eye – self-esteem. When in love, we tend to view ourselves through the eyes of the loved one. It's human nature. You may think that you're beautiful, talented, smart, etc., but if that person you love thinks otherwise, those negative thoughts can become contagious, and before you know it, you've internalized feelings of inadequacy. What's worse is that some people will purposely try to destroy your self- esteem to keep you wondering if you're worthy. Or to keep you in a state of desperately *trying* to be worthy. They'll intentionally do it to safeguard their own agenda. If a man wants to keep you under his thumb while he does whatever he wants on the side, he has to make you feel like you need to stay. He has to make you doubt your own worth and ability to walk away, so he will campaign for your insecurities. There are actually people in the world who consciously set out to do this! Self-esteem is self-explanatory; it comes from *self*. No one can give it to you and no one can take it from you unless you allow it to be taken. Sure, a person may have a plan to make you feel worthless so you won't go find better, but what is stopping you from simply walking away? It will always come back to *self.*

One day, Bryson and I decided to visit his mom house to spend some time with her. He went outside to play football with his nephew and to work on his truck while I talked and laughed with his mother inside for a while. She was very understanding and wasn't judgmental, so we talked about a lot of everything. Somehow, one of my ex-boyfriends came up in the conversation. Bryson and my ex-boyfriend grew up in the same neighborhood, and his mother and I were laughing about a funny story about when my ex and Bryson were kids. We were having a good time until Bryson walked in the room. His mother asked him why he didn't tell her about that comical incident years before when it happened. When Bryson heard my ex's name, he flipped out.

"Really Bianca, you gone talk about this n**** at my mother's house?" Bryson yelled.

I was so shocked at the way he overreacted. His mother tried to calm him down, but he kept ranting and raving about me bringing up my ex-boyfriend to his mother. I couldn't believe he was disrespecting me in front of his own mother. I stood up, grabbed my baby, and went to his truck. I was so pissed off and ready to go. I was so sick of his childishness and disgusting attitude. I was beginning to feel like nowhere was safe – if he would disrespect me in front of his own mother, he'd do it anywhere. His mother apologized to me, and I told her not to worry about it because it was not her fault. She was so embarrassed. On the way to his house, he asked me if I missed my ex so much that I had to mention him to his mother. My ex-boyfriend was the last person on my mind; his name was only brought up to tell a funny story from years ago. My explanation went in one of Bryson's ears and out the other. He had no intentions of actually listening to me. Eventually, I simply ignored him and sat in silence as he continued his tirade.

When we arrived back at his place, he was still going. His mouth was non-stop, and I was so tired of listening to him. I could feel myself getting more agitated with his voice with each passing second, but I tried ignoring him. Even when he walked up to me yelling and cursing, I didn't react. I didn't want to entertain his nonsense. I think my lack of a reaction is what set him off. He grabbed my arms and pushed me to the wall, still asking me why I mentioned my ex at his mother's house. He had a good grip and I yelled at him to let me go. At some point, his son walked past us and began screaming and crying. Bryson finally let me go and rushed after his son, yelling at him to be quiet and to stop being dramatic. While Bryson was in the kids' room trying to get them to calm down, I was looking for my phone. I'd never seen him this angry and I didn't want to stick around and let him hurt me. I couldn't find my phone, but I saw his phone.

Just as I was about to call 911, he came in and snatched the phone from me. He grabbed me and pushed me so hard, I stumbled backwards and almost fell to the ground. He was yelling at me about the phone, asking me what I was doing. Shocked by his actions, I didn't know what to do or say. I tried to walk away towards his room to get out of the kid's sight and wrap my mind around what was happening, but he came after me. He was yelling and pushed me to the doorway of his room, scaring the kids. I turned towards him and he pushed me so hard I flew from the doorway to the bed, and then down to the floor. He came into the room and slammed the door behind him. Before I could get up, he was on top of me with his hand up like he was going to hit me. I yelled at him over and over, begging him not to hit me. He finally got off me and sat on the floor next to me.

The whole night, I replayed in my head the events that transpired. Hours later, I was still shocked it went that far. Bryson was apologizing and trying to talk about what had happened all night, but I was too emotionally drained to process what he was trying to say. We slept in the same bed, but I was so uncomfortable. Every time he moved or got up, I was looking over my shoulder. I was so shaken up from what happened.

The next day, he was still apologizing. I began to think he was legitimately mentally unstable. I started to think he was a little off. I started feeling like I just did not like him as a person. The things he did were not just mistakes, they were just embedded in who he was as a man. I had so many regrets, and I wished I had really taken at look at his character long before getting into a serious relationship with him. I felt so embarrassed and weak. I kept wondering what I could've done during that moment to prevent this man from humiliating me. He begged me not to leave. I forgave him for his behavior, but I knew from then on that nothing would ever be the same. Every day for about a month, I thought about what happened. It kept replaying in my head. Every time an argument or a disagreement arose, I was afraid that it would lead to that point again. Every time he raised his voice, it reminded me of what happened.

I sat down and really started thinking about the quality and nature of my relationship. Why was I dealing with disrespect? We had different morals and values, so how could I really expect things to work with this man? Everything started getting the best of me - his friends, his job, his parenting, his ways, and the dumb choices he made. All of his friends were cheaters, womanizers, deceivers, woman beaters and childish. They were all lost, and I hated their negative influence on him. As long as he dealt with them, he could never be right and do right. At his job, there was always some mess involving other women. Women would commute all the way from the other side of town just let him cut their hair. Yes, a lot of people travel to get a great haircut, but I know fake when I see it. He even admitted that some of the women could care less about him cutting their hair; they just wanted to flirt with him. In regards to his children, there was nothing he wouldn't do for them financially, but they needed more than that. He needed to spend more time nurturing, guiding and bonding with them. His son is now about twelve years old and needs a real man in his life to show him the way. His daughter is about ten years old and she needs to see an example of how a real man should treat a woman. She needs to know what to tolerate and what to not tolerate from a man. He's even admitted that if his daughter met a man like himself, he would hate it. That mentality of knowing he could be better, but still not doing the right thing is a clear indication of his selfishness and preoccupation with the ways of the world. Sometimes he yelled and cursed at the children so harshly that I would have to step in to diffuse the situation. Every time things didn't go Bryson's way, he would have a fit. Sometimes it could be the simplest things that triggered him.

Every time something terrible happened between us, he would always beg me to stay. Every time I forgave him, he still would find a way to mess up. Our entire relationship was full of stress, drama and lies. He was still so jealous, and it always made me very uncomfortable. When he'd see me looking attractive or wearing clothes that somewhat revealed my shape, he would stare at me with this look like he was upset that I looked good. After getting off work or coming home from school, he would ask me if anyone tried to talk to me. He didn't want me to get a male personal trainer or even sign up for a gym membership at all. Instead of being proud of my looks, or complimenting me, he tried to stifle it or make me hide it at all times.

I was so tired and exasperated with him. I had no desire to sleep with him, and I was barely coming over to his house. I stopped complaining as much as I once did. I found myself cursing more and more at him. Sometimes, he was shocked by the things I said because he knew it was out of character. It became much harder to be thoughtful and considerate towards him.

I suppose I was still hanging in there waiting for something to magically happen. I was hoping he would one day say he scheduled a counseling session for us. I was wishing he would one day tell me about a plan he made to help us take steps to try to stick together and build our relationship. Of course, that day never came.

There will be time in life when you encounter people who are so broken, so emotionally and mentally sick that in order for them to shine, they have to steal some of your light. Whenever you're dealing with someone who sees you doing well, looking good, or just trying to live your best life, and the first reaction they have is negative, it's not about you. You haven't done anything wrong. You are not less than what you thought. In relationships, there are people who will see you with a new hairstyle, getting in shape, going back to school, getting a promotion, purchasing a new car or home, and they will make you feel like you are on top of the world. This person will be your biggest cheerleader, and if they're not on your level, they will feel inspired to *get* on your level and will let you show them how to have similar results and blessings. And then… there is the person who can't stand to see you looking good, doing well, making more money, trying a new style or stepping out and elevating your life. It's not because they just can't stand you or don't want you to be great. It's that your spotlight shines too much light on where they are lacking and they can't handle it. They may feel like they can't get on your level or achieve what you're achieving, so what they do is either pretend like what you're doing is not so great, or they try to get YOU to believe you shouldn't do all that elevating. After they plant a seed in your ear with the little things they say, they will have you thinking, "Maybe this *isn't* the right time to buy a new car", "Maybe this hairstyle *doesn't* look that good on me" or "Maybe I *am* wasting time and money at the gym." Be careful of those who feel so dim that they have to come after your light and dim yours too. That's not love.

My son's first birthday was approaching and it was time for his first haircut. Bryson and I were so excited. I was anticipating being able to experience that moment with my son. I wondered how he would act when he heard the clippers. Bryson was excited because he was a barber and he couldn't wait to put his personal touch on his son's head. Bryson was talking about cutting his hair for weeks and it was finally time. One of Bryson's shortcomings was his lack of patience. He could never wait to do things; it was like he had to jump and do whatever was on mind right away. He called or texted me saying he was going to cut his hair without me being there. He didn't want to wait until I get off work or got out of class. He just wanted to cut his hair when he felt like it without being considerate of me being able to witness it as well. One day, he called to tell me he was going to cut our son's hair, but I was home taking nap after an exhausting day of work. I woke up to see a video of my son getting his hair cut. I was so upset because I wanted to be there to share that moment with him. There were so many other incidents where Bryson took treasured moments from me because of his selfishness and impatience. The crazy part about it was that Bryson didn't understand my perspective; he didn't see the problem at all. The time I spent with him was rapidly decreasing.

I was due for an annual Well Woman's exam and finally took time out of my day to make an appointment. I was on the phone with Bryson when I parked my car in the parking lot of the doctor's office. He asked me how long it takes to receive the results. His question was so bizarre that I immediately began to feel anxiety. Why would he be worried about such a thing? I'd slept with Bryson a short time before the appointment, and I was a little afraid of getting the results to testing. I didn't trust him, and there was no telling what he'd been doing on the side. I got tested for multiple sexually transmitted diseases and even requested to be tested for the sexual transmitted diseases and infections that are not routinely part of a Well Woman's exam. Knowing the man I was dealing with, I needed that peace of mind. Once the appointment was over, I had to wait a few days for the results.

While hanging out with Bryson one day at his house, the doctor's office called with the results. Even though I was halfway asleep, the phone call alerted me because I know doctors typically only call when they need to deliver bad news. If everything was okay, there would be no reason to contact me. The doctor said everything was okay except that I tested positive for a sexually transmitted disease. The doctor went on to provide me with treatment information. I can honestly say that I wasn't shocked at the news. God had spoken to me several times about this man, but I never listened.

Bryson came back into the room and knew something was wrong from the look on my face. I asked him if there was anything he needed to tell me. Of course, being the type of man who would never own up to anything, he said no. I went on to tell him the doctor's news, and he went nuts. He was yelling and talking about how there was no way I could put that on him. Inside, I was thinking, *dude just tell the truth.* He was going back and forth with me, telling me how he's never had a sexual transmitted disease before. He said a lot of other things, trying to find his way out of his lies again. I just sat there and didn't waste any energy debating and arguing with him. In a way, I felt like I deserved whatever was happening to me because I should've left him long before it got to that point. Once he realized I wasn't paying him any mind, he finally confessed that he did have sexual relations with someone. For all I knew, it could've been multiple women.

I stuck around for about two and a half months after it happened. It felt like I was only there with him because we had already been together so long. I was used to being around him, dealing with him, settling, and being afraid of making a major change in my life. I knew deep down that we were just not going to work because he couldn't seem to change his ways. As time passed, it became easier for me to let go and let God. I had to hang it up.

This time, my move felt different. I was ready for what God had in store for me. I missed Bryson a lot, and every time he came to pick up our son, it was hard for me. Sometimes he'd bring his older two kids along, and that made me sad too. It was hard seeing them drive off without me, but I knew what was best for me. I had to let him go so he could grow. I wasn't teaching him anything by staying with him.

Bryson was slowly leading me to an early grave. Dealing with him was wreaking havoc on my self-esteem. Sometimes I thought I wasn't attractive or fun enough. I started to believe maybe I just wasn't enough for him. I thought the weight I'd gained from my son pushed him away from me. I was going crazy! I allowed this man to twist my mind up in so many ways. All relationships experience struggle, and I never expected perfection, but some things should just not be tolerated.

ca ca ca

CHAPTER 6
Just When I Thought I Was Done

A good friend of mine who lived in Baltimore, Maryland was having a baby shower. She was very supportive of everything I did, so I had to make sure I supported her in this milestone. I planned the trip and booked flights for my mother, sister and son. Our plan was to visit Washington D.C. and Virginia as well. Although I hadn't dealt with Bryson for a while, I hated that I didn't include him on the trip. It bothered me so much because traveling was the type of thing I wanted to share with him. He'd never been on a plane before. Out of the goodness of my heart, I just couldn't leave him out and told him about the trip. He hesitated, but I told him not to worry and to pack his bags. He agreed. Making that decision turned out to be a terrible mistake. He spent the trip being insecure and rude. Same old tune! He embarrassed me in front of my mother and we argued just about the entire time.

On one of the nights in the hotel room, I received a direct message on Instagram from a woman I didn't know. The message read, "nice body." I checked out her Instagram page and she didn't look familiar to me at all. I didn't understand why she was writing me – it felt random and strange. While Bryson and I were arguing, he took my phone and read my direct messages. He asked who the girl was, and I told him I had no idea. He left it alone.

On our way back to Houston, Bryson kept apologizing about how he'd ruined most of the trip for me. I forgave him, and we decided to work on being in a relationship again. I was happy to have my Bryson back. I tried my best to put everything that we'd went through in the past, so that we could move forward. Things were going pretty well until I noticed that something didn't feel physically right about my body. I know my body, and nine times out of ten, when I sense a problem, I'm right. I went to the doctor to get tested for multiple sexually transmitted diseases. Bryson came to the doctor with me, and I could tell by his body posture, the tone in his voice, and the look on his face that he'd messed up. I just knew it. I found out that I had a bacterial infection. When we got back to the car, he told me he wanted to discuss some things with me. He revealed that he needed to take a blood test because he may have another baby. My heart dropped. I couldn't believe it. A baby? *Really?* The crazy part was that he told me the girl who randomly messaged me during our vacation was the woman who may have had his baby. He went on to tell me that he'd slept with other women as well. He claimed all of this happened before we left town for our trip. I didn't want to hear anything else he had to say. I just wanted to get away from him as soon as possible. He kept trying to talk to me about it, but I didn't want to hear it. He kept apologizing to me, promising that if I ever forgave him, he'd be the best man to me that he'd ever been. Time passed, and what did I do? I was right back with him.

Why do people stay in situations that are damaging to their dignity, self-worth, and even their physical health? False hope and anticipation can cause an individual to wait around dangerous circumstances for something amazing to happen, and they often just end up getting hurt. If a person has not shown you concrete changes towards changing, what is the benefit of sticking around? Because words are cheap, and anyone can simply say they love you or that they're going to change or improve something. It requires commitment to actually put those words into actions. There are two types of cheaters out there – the sneaky ones who step out from time to time but keep it hidden away and quiet so as not to disturb their main loved one's life, money, health, dignity, etc., and the messy type who is willing to risk it all for the sake of a few moments between the sheets with someone who provides a temporary thrill. The latter person will compromise your health, happiness and emotional well-being. The latter person won't even think enough of you to protect you from whatever exposure may be transferred during the act of deception. If that person is not protecting you and your well-being, and *you* are not protecting your own well-being enough to walk away, then who is left to protect you?

A couple of months after Bryson promised to do right by me, I began to believe in my heart that he wasn't involved with other women. He was home more often and more engaged in quality time. The problem was that he felt that not dealing with other women was all it took to satisfy me. I understand that it's a major accomplishment for a cheater to stop cheating and commit to someone but refraining from cheating alone will not keep me. I still had to deal with Bryson being disrespectful and unappreciative. I still had to hear him complaining all the time. I got so tired of it. After all that happened, he still hadn't gotten his act together. I was at the point where I just didn't want him touching me, and I couldn't stand to be around him.

It was Christmas 2017. The day went well. Throughout the day, Bryson and I were talking about spending some quality time together once we'd get home and put the kids in bed. When the time came, I just wasn't in the mood. It didn't feel like Bryson was matching my effort in the relationship. He didn't seem to understand that there was much more to be repaired in our relationship besides not cheating. Being faithful, for him, was major because he'd cheated in all of his past relationships. By this point, I needed to be shown why I should stay with him. He raised so much hell over the fact that I didn't want to sleep with him that night and told me I needed to get out of his house if I wasn't going to do it. Throughout the entire argument, I had been laying down, but when he told me to get out of his house, I got up abruptly. It was after midnight, but I didn't care and started getting my things together to leave. I was just sick of listening to him yell and curse me. I had no more patience for the disrespect. He talked me into staying, but I stood my ground and didn't allow him to touch me at all.

CRCRCR

CHAPTER 7
Put My Foot Down

I had to leave Bryson. Trying to be with him was exhausting every area of my life. The stress kept building and building until it was threatening to spill over. I couldn't handle it. I left the day after Christmas. We argued in front of his daughter. She started crying, I was crying, and hated everything about it. I couldn't stand to see her crying, due to our arguing; it was just too dysfunctional of a situation to maintain. I tried to get Bryson to relax and stop arguing in front of his child. He didn't understand - he kept going on and on. The more he lashed out, the easier he made it for me to walk away. In the past, I'd never left him and stayed gone for too long without entertaining him in some way. This time it had to be different. I had to show him that if he couldn't appreciate, respect, and treat me how I was supposed to be treated, I couldn't be with him at all. Deep down, I didn't want to leave him, but it's almost like he forced my hand with the way he treated me.

I stood my ground. When Bryson texted me about things that had nothing to do with our son, I ignored him. Every time he tried to convince me that we should be back together, I ignored him. Besides, he didn't seem sincere about the things that he was saying anyway. Every time we'd broken up, he had a list of go-to promises and catchphrases he'd say to win me back. I didn't want to hear the talking anymore. I wanted him to *do* something! Stop talking and start walking! That did not happen. The communication slowed down a lot. I had to consistently remind myself to be strong.

൩൩൩

CHAPTER 8
Valentine's Day

It was Valentine's Day. I couldn't believe I was going to be spending it without Bryson, and it bothered me so much. He texted me at about five o'clock in the morning on that day, letting me know he was available to babysit if I had something to do. I know Bryson - I knew that wasn't all he wanted to know. He wanted to know if I had something planned. He was being insecure. I didn't give him the satisfaction of knowing. Instead, I thanked him but said I would not need a babysitter. That evening, I went out to eat with my sister and my son. I can't lie - I was bothered, but I had to stay strong. Bryson and I had previously discussed that he would pick up our son that evening since I had to work extremely early that next day. He agreed to drop him off with my aunt instead, so I wouldn't have to drive to the other side of town at 4 o'clock in the morning. While we were out eating, Bryson called me. He was angry that I was out at dinner. He asked me if I had another man around our son.

Bryson came to pick up our son later that night. We ended up discussing a few things. He told me he'd been casually seeing someone, and I told him that I'd had a few conversations of my own here and there with guys, but nothing serious. It didn't phase me that he'd been talking to someone because were human and that's just reality. It was time for him to go. He gave me a hug, and we couldn't resist one another. I missed him so much. We kissed, and before I realized what I'd gotten myself into, we slept together. After that, I assumed we were going to be together. I just knew he was going to drop this woman he'd been seeing so that we could work on being together again. We started talking on the phone a lot. We went out to the movies and had a good time. We went to a bar to have drinks one night, and he told me he was going to tell her about us so that we could focus on repairing our relationship. We slept together again.

Days passed, and Bryson kept hesitating about telling this woman about us getting back together. He kept going on and on about how I left him, ignored him, and didn't give him a chance. I constantly explained to Bryson the reason why I left him and ignored him, but he didn't seem to understand at all. We hung out a few more times. He started becoming distant, taking a long time to text me back at times, ignoring my calls here and there. He acted like I did something wrong to him. I didn't understand. He finally admitted to me that he allowed this woman to meet his two oldest children. That shocked me! I started realizing that he must have been developing feelings for this woman. That was the only way to explain why he'd feel compelled to introduce her to his children. How could he be so into a woman that he barely knew? We broke up at the end of December, and I found out less than two months later that he was going on family outings with another woman! *Where they do that at?* I was hurt and confused. I wanted answers, but he wasn't giving them to me. He acted like he just didn't care about a thing. He seemed confused about whether he wanted to be with me or her. We argued constantly about what his next move was going to be.

It was Bryson's day to pick up our son. He didn't show up. He didn't answer any calls or texts that day from me. It was very strange and unlike Bryson to not show up on his day, and extremely strange for me not to hear from him at all. I became very worried. Was he with this woman? Was he acting selfish and silly due to what we were going through? The next morning when I got up for work, I still hadn't heard from him. I called him a few times on my way to work. Still, nothing. There was a major car wreck on my normal route to work and traffic was at a standstill. My mind was going 100 mph. I called my job and told them I was going to be late. I decided to pop up at Bryson's house to see what in the world was going on. I got to his house and saw the living room light on. My heart was racing fast. When I knocked on the door, the light went off. I called his phone again. No answer. I stayed there for a few minutes knocking on the door every couple of seconds and no answer. Finally, I gave up and started walking to my car. I heard Bryson's front door open, and I turned around. He was standing there with the door cracked. He seemed to be taking things for a joke. He was laughing and asking me what I was doing at his house. Angrily, I started walking to my car to leave. He ran over to me, grabbed me, and he apologized. He said he wanted me to stay. We slept together again.

Before I was planning to go back to work, I went to the doctor's office to get a note for work. I thought it was going to be quick, that I'd be in and out and on my way back to work. That didn't happen. The doctor ran all kinds of test on me. The doctor told me I was very dehydrated and my heart rate was very close to being abnormal. I barely ate or drank anything for two days before I went to the doctor. I was so stressed that I hadn't realized I wasn't eating and drinking as I should. I had to stay in the emergency room overnight, so the doctor could monitor me.

I started to lose my mind. I lost focus. I found myself crying and breaking down too often. I wasn't performing well at work. I was getting to work late. I was doing my homework assignments for school at the last minute and barely passing assignments. I stopped working out as much as I used to. I couldn't wrap my head around the way Bryson was going about things. My emotions were all over the place. And then, I got completely out of character; I found the girl Bryson was talking to on Instagram. I direct messaged her to drop the bomb that Bryson and I had slept together multiples times. I told her a few other private things that I thought would shock her. I thought that telling her that and possibly ruining their relationship would've made me feel better, but it didn't. In the end, I felt stupid, and on top of that, Bryson was showing me that he didn't care not one bit. He began acting like he didn't want me at all. I couldn't understand why a woman he'd supposedly only known for two months already met his children. I couldn't understand why he seemed to want a serious relationship with her. I didn't even know how to process all of this; it just wasn't registering in my head. I didn't understand how he would even have a thought of starting over with someone else after all we'd been through together. I couldn't help but feel like there was nothing left to hold onto and to just let go. I never had the luxury of security with Bryson. He never reassured me that he had my back, that he'd never let another woman come between us, or anything of that nature. His actions made me feel the opposite, as if I was just one the many women he juggled. His negativity didn't help matters either. It was almost impossible to get through to him. When he didn't have his way, he'd hang up in my face, get loud and aggressive, avoid conversations, and run away from his responsibilities. The entire situation was stealing my joy, and I was tired. Because I loved him so much and wanted what was best for him, I decided to let God deal with him. It was out of my control.

It has been proven time and time again that human beings typically want what they feel they cannot have. Sometimes, it's not the actual object or person that drives them – it's the triumph of acquiring something that felt out of reach. This is why when one person throws in the towel and walks away, the other person tries to hold on for dear life. This is why when one person refuses to be pulled into the relationship, the other person goes crazy trying to figure out how to get back in good graces. Even toddlers don't like being told "no," and will throw full-blown temper tantrums when that toy they want is within sight, but not within reach. You have to always have enough strength to walk away and stay away if necessary to protect your peace of mind and physical well-being. Otherwise, that person you deem to be the love of your life may grow too content and comfortable. That person may push the envelope more and more, just to see how much you'll stick around to tolerate. It's a chasing game. The person doing the chasing wins. When you walk away from a toxic situation that does not fulfill you, and the other person shapes up to make the necessary changes to get you back, they are chasing, so you win. When you stick around, spending your days ringing that person's phone off the hook, following them to see where they are, investigating to see who they're with, you lose. And if you are in a situation where you are waiting for the love of your life to make a decision between you and another person, you lose BIG TIME. Because even if you are the choice, in the end, you still handed the power over to that person to either accept or reject you. No human being should have that level of power over you. To sit around twiddling your thumbs like a contestant on a dating show, giving that person the opportunity to weigh his or her options is not how love works! If you love yourself, you would not be satisfied with being one of the options; you would only accept being the *only* option.

CHAPTER 9
The Dream

On March 26, 2018, I woke up from a dream that I believe was a message from God. The dream started with Bryson, his date, which was the famous Gabrielle Union, and a few others sitting at a restaurant dining table. For some reason, I left the table for a moment. When I returned, everyone who was there originally was gone. Instead, there were about three Hispanic males at the table. They looked like the typical appearance of gang members, and their hands were covered in blood. I remember running away from them, out into the middle of the street in broad daylight. I tried to run away repeatedly, but they continued to catch up with me. The crazy part was that every time I started running from them, I felt like I was running at a good speed and putting significant distance between us, but when they caught up with me, it was like I started running in slow motion. It felt like I was using all my strength, trying hard to run as fast as possible, but I couldn't speed up. Something was weighing me down.

I couldn't figure it out. The closer they got to me, the more afraid I became. The ironic part of it all was that every time they caught up with me, they passed me up.

I woke up at 5:09am, quickly got dressed, and I was on the way to work by 5:20am. The dream stayed on my mind. As I was riding to work, I asked God to reveal his message to me. Here is what I think God was trying to tell me:

The night of the dream, I went to sleep in a worried state, just as I had for weeks prior to the dream. In the dream, I remember feeling uncomfortable, hurt, and confused sitting at the table watching Bryson with another woman. Yet, I remained sitting there, accepting what was going on right in front of my face. After seeing the woman on Instagram who Bryson had been involved with, I started beating myself up. On Instagram, she appeared to be a very pretty woman. I started wondering if he wanted her because he thought she looked better than me, or because I still hadn't lost all the weight after giving birth to our child. All kinds of insecure thoughts were plaguing my mind. I felt like God used Gabrielle Union in my dream because she is a very pretty woman as well. He was trying to tell me to stop beating myself up, running from the truth, and accept people and circumstances for who and what they are. I had to check myself. I had to know and believe that no matter what anyone says or thinks, I am beautiful. I had to love myself for who I am - the way God made me- and be comfortable and confident in my skin. I had to realize that there's no woman or man I'd ever have to compete with, regardless of how they look or what they possess. It was time I stop running from the truth and face the reality of how this man treated me and what I'd experienced and endured with him. Running away from my problems and refusing to deal with the truth would have me running for the rest of my life, and my problems would still catch up with me. The more I ran from my problems, the more I felt weighed down. In the dream, those three men represented my problems, but they passed me up when it came time to attack me. God was saying, "These problems are not for you; you're only dealing with these problems because you're choosing to deal with the problems. Stop running!" God said, "Accept that this man may not be the man for you. He may not be your husband, he may not be the man that wants to change his life around and be with you, he may not be the man to put you and his family first, and he may not be ready for what you have to offer." Another thing I took from the dream is that I needed to look at myself in the mirror. I thought, *Am I really wife material? I want this man to settle down and marry me, but am I worth it? How can I be with someone if I'm emotionally unstable?* Sometimes we get a little too ahead of ourselves and don't even realize that some of what we need to correct and build is within us. I had to stop running and fight. I had to stop running, be at peace, and let things be.

There is no rhyme or reason to matters of the heart. If love were a logical thing that could be predicted and calculated, it could be determined that the person who puts in the time and hard work in a relationship will come out on the other side with the success story, right? Wrong! The only thing in your control is how you love yourself. You might have weathered the storm with someone, built them up, and invested in them. And still, you may wake up one day to find that person you've loved for so long on the arm of someone else. But none of that has to do with how you feel about yourself. None of that makes you any less beautiful or worthy. As soon as you stop looking to others to measure that beauty and worth, you will see that you held the ruler in your own hands all along.

CRCRCR

CHAPTER 10
Why Did I Stay So Long?

The main reason I stayed with Bryson so long is because I lacked the knowledge I needed to be in a successful, healthy relationship. Being young and naive, I lacked the tools and self-assurance to see him for who and what he was. If I had been wiser, it would have been a very short-lived relationship. Because all the red flags were there; I simply chose to settle and deal with the issues out of fear and contentment. Much of my fear stemmed from the thought of him with someone else. So I stayed and allowed myself to be mistreated and controlled.

Although I have a lot of negative memories about Bryson, there were a few good things I enjoyed that helped to justify the bad times. Bryson could be fun to be around because he had a comical nature. He was always very well-dressed and groomed; I'd never met a man who was just as clean as me. He kept his house and car super clean. He got satisfaction from seeing the lines the vacuum cleaner formed on the carpet. He just had an all-around high standard for how he took care of his home, his belongings and himself. He did, however, develop a problem spending his money on clothes, shoes, and other unnecessary things, but he always managed to pay his bills. If his children needed anything, he would always do his best to provide.

Bryson was also very passionate. He loved cuddling, kissing for long periods of time, and showing affection. Although it was temporary, he knew how to really make me feel loved. On his good days, he had a way of being very loving.

But, Bryson knew how to be very manipulative and deceiving. He lied so much that it was natural for him. Lies rolled off the tip of his tongue without thought. With most people, you can usually tell they are lying due to their change in expression, gestures, or even voice. Bryson was the same whether he was lying or telling the truth. He lied with absolutely no remorse. I never fully believed Bryson, but he made those lies seem so real – almost like he truly believed what he was saying.

Our son and family played a major role in holding onto the relationship. There were times when we broke up, but sharing a son created opportunities for us to come back together in multiple ways. I can remember incidents when I dropped my son off or went to pick him up and ending up hanging out at Bryson's house. There were other times when Bryson called me on FaceTime, with the pretense of checking on our son, but really wanting to talk to me.

I also didn't want to deal with people knowing about our breakup. It was so embarrassing to be asked about him. It was humiliating for people to know that we weren't in a happy relationship. I was also embarrassed in front of those few family members who knew that we were constantly in and out of a relationship. I imagine that they often wondered why we just couldn't get it right.

I loved Bryson genuinely. I was so committed to him that it almost seemed unreal. I didn't give any other man a chance. I was blind to other options. I was so caught up on Bryson's potential that I couldn't see that he was showing me exactly who he was all along. I was so caught up on how I envisioned things could be between us that I kept trying to force it work.

ରେ ରେ ରେ

CHAPTER 11
Letting Go

I tried so many different things to try to save my relationship. But Bryson was showing me he didn't want it to be saved. His actions made it obvious that repairing our relationship was not a priority, because he was always messing up. When I suggested counseling, there was always some kind of excuse. He always procrastinated when it came to taking steps for us to move forward. He always said he would be willing to try counseling, but he never actually followed through on it. At one point, he even initiated the counseling and reached out to a pastor. But then he kept messing up before our appointment, so I decided against it altogether.

The realization I had to face was that dealing with Bryson was bad for me. No matter my efforts or how good of a woman I was to him, he just wasn't ready for me. Whether it was me or another woman, he just wasn't ready to be a real man and have real love. At times, he tried to blame his ways on his upbringing and the fact that he didn't have his father in his life. But as a grown man, he should know better. I'm the 3rd woman to have a child with him, and if he doesn't find ways to learn, grow and change, he'll be on his 5th or more, still doing the same old thing. Deep down inside, I knew he just wasn't ready to be what was required of him in a monogamous, adult relationship, but it was still hard to completely let go because I loved him genuinely.

One night, after having an argument with Bryson over the phone, I was so hurt and bothered that I got down on my knees beside my bed, spread my arms out, tilted my head back, closed my eyes, and I began to pray to God. Tears rolled down my face as I asked Him for guidance and strength to stand my ground. That night, I knew letting go was the best thing for me. I felt relieved and excited about what life could be without carrying the stress of that toxic relationship on my back.

It was time to bring the best out of me. I became more focused in every aspect of my life. I started working on my book. I believe God not only put me through past situations to be lessons, but also to be a blessing by sharing my testimony. I started researching the steps toward opening a salon and breaking into real estate investing. Without so much time spent on a dysfunctional relationship, I found the time to truly explore my aspirations.

Since the birth of my son, I'd been unhappy with the weight I gained. I finally had time to join a gym; investing in my personal health became a priority for me to live my best life. I developed and followed a meal plan to control my calorie intake, set goals to increase my water intake each day, and I started seeing positive results. Sometimes, meal prepping was time-consuming, but I made it happen. With each passing day, I looked and felt better.

Throughout the drama in my relationship with Bryson, I was not able to really focus on my school work. Once I let him go, I started earning A's on all my assignments. Even with a hectic schedule, I had more than enough time for school work. When I was with Bryson, it felt like I never had time to do anything. And even if I did have free time, my morale was so low, I was rarely in the mood to accomplish anything while I was with him.

It was time to get to greatness. I will never again allow a man to hinder my blessings or hold me back from my purpose. I started attending church more often and drew closer and closer to God. From that night I dropped to my knees and praised God, I knew my breakthrough was coming. I knew God was about to really show out in my life. I didn't know when or how, but I didn't care because I knew my blessings were going to come right on time. I had to let that hurt go!

CRCRCR

CHAPTER 12
The Lesson

I've learned so many things since the day I received that direct message on Instagram from Bryson. I had to learn the hard way, but I learned.

1. Always Keep God your number one priority

When God is your number one priority, everything else in life will fall into place. Several times, I found myself wondering why God allowed certain things to happen to me. I had to check myself and stop questioning God's work. Everything happens for a reason. When you have faith in God, you don't worry, you're at peace, and you know God is working in your favor.

2. Teach people how to treat you

When you allow someone to lie, cheat, or disrespect you in any way, you have to let them know it's not acceptable that very first time. You have to call them out on whatever they've done. You may even have to keep your guard up until that person proves to you that they can be trusted or until you feel comfortable with allowing them to be back in your space. If you don't stand your ground, people will repeatedly mistreat you. Know your breaking point. Know your worth. You must protect your well-being and your peace.

3. Your business is not everybody's business

You have to watch who you allow in your circle and what you share with them. Everybody does not need to know your business. It's human nature to feel like you just have to vent to others about what you're going through, but you really have watch who you're talking to and what you're talking about around them. Some people will give you their poor advice and lead you to make terrible decisions. Some people are so negative. Negative energy is transferable, and you have to block that negative energy. The best advice you can get comes from the good book, the Bible!

4. Forgive

Learning to forgive is key to living in peace. Holding grudges does nothing but weigh you down. When you forgive someone for something that they've done, make sure you forget as well. The worst thing you can do is make someone feel like they are locked in a jail cell. No one wants to feel that way. No one wants to continuously hear about the wrong they've done. Forgive and forget or forgive and move on.

How did this all benefit me?

Being in a toxic relationship and dealing with all that came with it helped me become a better person overall. I grew stronger, wiser, more independent, more understanding, and closer to God. I've grown so much that sometimes it surprises even me. Prior to meeting Bryson, I was on my way to destruction. God had to do something to get my attention. While navigating through the rocky relationship, I started seeking advice. I watched videos from life coaches and motivational speakers. I listened to sermons and gained a deeper understanding of life. I learned to let go and let God!

ଔଔଔ

www.ingramcontent.com/pod-product-compliance
Lightning Source LLC
LaVergne TN
LVHW021541080426
835509LV00019B/2774